The Inner Life

of

Love

P.J. Pennington

Balboa Press books may be ordered through booksellers or by contacting:

Balboa Press
A Division of Hay House
1663 Liberty Drive
Bloomington, IN 47403
www.balboapress.com
1 (877) 407-4847

Because of the dynamic nature of the Internet, any web addresses or links contained in this book may have changed since publication and may no longer be valid. The views expressed in this work are solely those of the author and do not necessarily reflect the views of the publisher, and the publisher hereby disclaims any responsibility for them.

Any people depicted in stock imagery provided by Thinkstock are models, and such images are being used for illustrative purposes only. Certain stock imagery © Thinkstock.

All photographs included in the interior were taken by or are the property of Pamela Joy Pennington, unless otherwise indicated. Author's photograph provided by Terri McKee Photography

1. Religion and spirituality, 2. Personal transformation and growth
3. Mysticism 4. Poetry and photos.

ISBN: 978-1-4525-1420-8 (sc)
ISBN: 978-1-4525-1421-5 (e)

Library of Congress Control Number: 2014908461

Printed in the United States of America.

Balboa Press rev. date: 06/04/2014

BALBOA.
PRESS
A DIVISION OF HAY HOUSE

I offer my gratitude, my love and my very being to
God the Compassion and the Merciful.

Contents

Acknowledgements

I thank God, the author of all inspiration and love.

I also acknowledge the inspiration of my guide Sidi, who often patiently awaited my listening ear. He encouraged me in writing the poetry of devotion.

My loving husband Todd, is my greatest supporter and source of optimism. He often believes I can do more than I imagined.

Thanks to my sons and their wives for the lessons they have taught me and the photos of and by them.

Special thanks to Susan Stoner (Author of the Sage Adair mysteries) for all of her assistance and encouragement. And thanks to Ra'ufa Sherry Tuell (author of *Islamic Approaches to Patient Care*) for her inspiration.

And finally, I offer thanks to God for surrounding me with many wonderful, caring, friends who help and support me and who share their lives with me. I hope they know how much they mean to me.

Introduction

I have written this book to challenge the reader to see with eyes beyond the physical and hear with the ears of the soul. I ask only that the reader be willing to approach God from the heart rather than any particular religious tradition. Let your soul see that the Originator of all things, our Beloved, invites us all into a relationship of intimacy and love.

Beloved is a word often used to describe a special or sacred association. What we see in the relationship of lovers is a metaphor for the relationship with the Divine. My Beloved, the Lover of my soul is the True Lover. My Beloved is also the author and giver of compassion, mercy, and love. It is my Beloved who fills my soul and gives words to the expressions in this book.

Another metaphor frequently used to describe our relationship with the Divine Mind, is the garden. The garden is the place of intimacy with God. There it is, that I am met by the Lover of my soul. We see in the garden, the flowers opening in response to the light. The garden, according to some traditions, is the place where first we joined the Beloved.

The ocean of God's love is an image of unimaginable depth and breadth. That love is both powerful and comforting, persistent and unyielding to opposition. God's love presses onward. I yield to the greatness of God's love because my life feels unfulfilled in resistance.

My spiritual path leads me on a quest of discovery. I seek to correctly know my authentic Self. I strive for the intimacy of a union with the Lover of my soul. The more I learn of myself and my Beloved, the more I experience this paradox: I am both blissfully content to simply be in my Beloved's presence and ever desirous of learning more.

The journey is about being honest with myself and who I am in order to recover an intimate relationship with God. It is about rediscovering God's light at the core of my being and how that knowledge influences my interactions with others. On the path of discovery I find that my life is concerned with attitudes. My attitudes dictate my actions.

My relationship with the Divine includes connection to humanity. Regardless of our beliefs or religious practices, we are all children of the same Creator. On this path of revelation, I have found that what unites humanity is so much greater than what divides us. As a child of God, living among other children of God, I find that all that really exists is God.

I will extend mercy and compassion the way I would want to receive it. We are all children of one God with many names and many descriptions. But there is only ONE. And I seek to discover all the aspects of that ONE.

While the words in this book may seem personal, it is the same message to us all. God is love. God is merciful and compassionate. God is closer than our thoughts. God speaks to us. God wants a relationship with us. God is in each one of us. We need only to open our hearts, to hear and experience God's love.

Though God, is neither male nor female, for ease of communication, I usually refer to God with the pronoun "He". In the poem "Who", I use both gender pronouns simply to make the point that God is, both and neither gender, and is all encompassing, without limitations.

I invite you the reader, to know the God within, who loves without measure and is the source of true peace. Let God be your Beloved.

Living in Love

I open my heart to be filled
With the love of God to overflowing.
May all people
Experience God's abundance.

In You I Exist

In You, O God, I have my being
I have nothing except you.
All love flows from you.
All sadness is consoled by you.

You clothe me in your righteous love.
You wrap me in your mercy.
I am dead, but you restore my life.
My joy exists in you alone.

When I am weary,
I lay my head upon your breast
And hear your heart which beats within me.
Your love restores my strength.

One day, when I am finished,
My travels through this land fulfilled,
I shall climb upon my boat
And row upon the sea of love.

The Clothes I Wear

These clothes I wear
Do not define me.
The qualities of my being
Shine through my speech and actions.
You may look at my skin, my hair, and my eyes
And think you know me.
You see that I am not part of your tribe.
And yet, I am not what I look like.
I am so much more.
You place labels that separate us from one another.
I *am* you. You *are* me.
We are one.
We love the same God.
There is no other god but God.
Nothing else exists but God.
There is ONLY ONE GOD!

Who?

Who is this Beloved One?
Who is the Cherished One that speaks to my heart,
With a deep longing to be known?
In the intimacy which only lovers share,
We are bound together through time and space.

She dwells within my heart,
And I abide in Hers.
No one understands me like my Beloved.
His essence lies with me.
My very essence is His.

Who is my Beloved?
If you do not know this Treasured One,
I can only try to describe the Light of my soul.
How can I find words to describe this love?
Everywhere I look
I see the face of my Eternal Lover.

"The Prophets are all brothers, and their Lord is one, and their Creator and
their message is one. All come from one father and mother."
*Shaykh Muhammad al-Jamal ar-Rifa'I as Shadhili

Now we see through a window dimly, but when we are reunited,
we shall see God face to face.
And we shall know God with the same clarity as we are known.
Paraphrased from I Cor. 13:12 (Bible)

Awaken My Beloved

Awaken my beloved. Do not slumber.
I am jealous for every moment with you.
Be not so busy with preparations that
Your eyes become clouded and heavy.
Do not sweep the floors.
But sweep away the cobwebs from your heart.
Awaken my beloved for I am calling.

Awaken! O awaken my beloved
To find me waiting for you!
I am the One your heart searches for.
I am here with you.
Awaken to the great love
Which swells through your being.
Awaken to the union between us.
Together our love flows toward new beginnings.

My Love

He is my only love
For all that exists is Him.
He is my source of joy.
There is no joy but Him.
In Him is strength to walk in this world.
There is no other Source of strength.

      Because I am His, I reveal His mercy.
      Because I am His, I demonstrate compassion.
      Because I am His, I *am* His love.
      His love is everything and I am His.
      I partake of His abundance
      Within the sweetness of His love.

My heart is eagerly open
To know all that He is.
My joy cannot be contained.
I speak his name and I am transported
To a love beyond imagination.
He speaks my name and we are ONE.

Be near me, o my God
That I may forever live as a reflection of your love.

Nearness

O God, my Beloved
Let my heart be not confused by man's thoughts.
But may my thoughts be your thoughts;
And my heart be yours.
Let my feet walk the path of righteousness.

When I call to you, hear me.
When I reach toward you,
Incline toward me.

You are closer than my heartbeat
Your breath is life to me.
Your love gives me purpose.
You are nearer to me than any other.

O God my Beloved
You are my joy and
I am yours.

Freedom

In God's great love, my heart soars like an eagle.
I am lifted up by the breath of God.
Hidden in the mountain of His love is a knowledge that sets me free.
I am wholly yielded to God's will. And in that surrender
I am freed from bondage,
Enjoined by peace.

MORE

There is so much more.
The words, which are true,
Might say one thing,
But if you look inside your heart
You will find a deeper truth.

Who is the one who speaks from within?
Who is the one you argue with,
When trying to justify your attitude?
Who is it that answers you with love?

Who is it that knows so much, much more,
Than what you think?
Tell me of the boundaries of the universe.
There is so much more.

There is one who lives within
And yet cannot be contained,
Whose thoughts created the reality
Of what you truly are.

When I believe I am alone, and that my decisions have no influence on others,
I deny the Source of life and love within me..

To See the Face of God

Much of my life was spent in loneliness.
It was not until I realized I am never alone,
That I discovered the faces of God all around me.
Looking in the mirror I see,
The face of God is staring back at me.
The man begging on the street corner,
Is perhaps an angel, encouraging my better nature.
The woman in the grocery store,
Yelling at her child
Could be a wounded version of me.
The old woman sitting alone in her room
That feels as if no one sees her,
Has forgotten her true identity.
The teacher, selflessly offering her life
For children, not her own, is God's.
Loneliness occurs when I forget
That God dwells within me.
He is closer than my thoughts.
And I am loved.

Beyond

All of this too, will fade from view.
All will become a meager memory within the mind.
What will remain?
That which always was; the Origin, the Source.

In my dream
I see another world.
Where nothing is impossible
And I am invincible.
Who dreams?

If I hold onto it really tightly
Can I make this life last longer?
Can I keep my soul within this vessel?
Can I live here forever?
Would I really want to?

What does this world hold for me
That is more beautiful than being with God?
Not even your embrace, my love,
Can hold me here when God calls my name.

I Am Home

I searched for you
Though you were never lost.
I thought I lost *my* way.
But you always knew exactly where I was.
I thought perhaps I was looking in the wrong place.
You were in every place.
I thought I needed to have a different practice.
You were in every practice.

I thought that perhaps I wasn't praying right.
You heard every prayer.
I thought perhaps I couldn't know until I died.
I had only to live, to open my eyes and see.
I *can* know the One who knows me.
My home lives within me.
I am home.

My Prayer

O my beloved,
I know that I do not always walk this path
In perfection.
I know that sometimes, in ignorance
I fall short.
I trust that in your mercy and love,
You will forgive my inadequacies.
I know that you will teach me to be the person
I am meant to be.

Because of your tender mercies and great love
Toward me,
I continue to rest into your guidance in order
To know you.
You are the one who holds my soul in your hands,
And my love.
You it is, that moves me.
I long to be an example of your love.
Help me to rest in you.
It is you who teaches me
To continuously express your mercy.

Behold the Shadow Self

by Dan Loranger

Those parts of me which I think no one sees,
Follow me around as shadows.

Sometimes I am the only one
That doesn't see
My wounded, judgmental, or angry self.

I try to hide my sensitivity
Thinking myself safe,
Because no one knows the real me.

When I am unwilling to appreciate
The whole of me;
Perceiving myself too flawed
To be loveable,
I deny the immeasurable love of God.

The Fountain of Peace

Let me drink deeply of His love
Let my thirst be quenched with peace.
Let me walk in the path of joy, which is
Defined by compassion and mercy.
I am refreshed.
I am at peace.
I surrender to the cleansing of my soul.
His love will motivate my actions.

Shadows Disappear

There was a time when my world closed in on me.
All that I could see was pain, sadness, fear and darkness.
Once the light penetrated the darkness
The dimness began to lose its power to conceal.
As the light grows in intensity from within
The shadows disappear.
What remains is what was always there:
Love, without boundaries, without measure;
Whole and complete, God within.
The causes of sadness and fear
Are seen for what they really are:
Illusion and misconceptions
God's love brings me out of the shadows
Of gloom and pain,
Into the light of his tenderness and mercy.

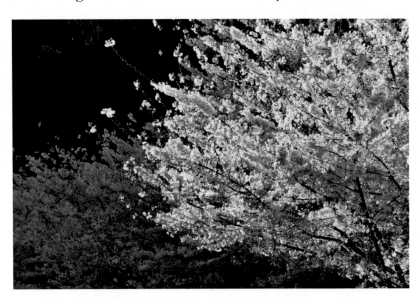

My Hope

Sometimes, it seems that life comes at me
With vengeance.
I can't find my way to the light.
All around me is darkness and despair.
While I know with some part of me
That God has not forgotten me,
I have forgotten what His voice
Of compassion and grace sound like.

God has not changed.
There is none greater.
God can bring me through the fire.
While the flames dance around me,
I will still give praises to the One
That is greatest.
And if the flames take my life
Let me die trusting in His deliverance;
Fully conscious of His love.
I take refuge in God the Generous,
The Protector of my soul,
And the supplier of great mercy.

Surrender

How can you possibly forgive me?
I have been so bull-headed.
And yet, there you are before me,
Open armed so to speak,
Treating me with infinite love and mercy.

My heart is moved toward you
And you engulf me in your love.
I am free!
I surrender all that I have
And all that I am.
From the depths of my heart
To the superficiality of my possessions,
Nothing is mine.

How can I even begin to consider
That I have anything else but you.
My possessions are less than dust.
There is nothing that shall keep me
From your great and expansive love.
Only you exist.

I am nothing without you.

God's love surrounds me and sustains me lifting me to new heights

My Beloved

When I behold your beauty
I am transfixed.
I want to open to your enduring love.
You continually beseech me
To follow you.
I have never trusted any
As I trust you, and yet
I am afraid to lose myself.
Your invitation pleads with me
To open myself to your tenderness.
Your supplications to yield to your affections
Pull at my heart.
If I give myself to you completely
What will remain of me?
Your passionate declarations come to me
Even in my sleep.
Your love gives my life purpose.
I can resist you no longer.
We will be one and revel in the glories of our devotion.
Our passions shall fill the universe,
And in my complete surrender to your affections,
You surrender also to mine and we are one.
I am fulfilled. I am at peace. No one else exists

Holiness

Why do I come to you in prayer?
Is it for you to understand me?
Or is it for me?
Why do I pour out my heart in supplication?
Why do I wash my outer self? Why fast?
Do you need for me to cease my self-indulgences?
Does it change one thing about your love for me?
You know my sentiments before
I lay them before you.
What must be cleansed is my heart,
And anything that steals my love away from you.
Reciting holy words is not for your sake,
But to remind me that you are ever near.
You are the compassionate one.
I deny myself that I might *be* compassion
For those who enjoy little.
We are one.
The outward expressions must be
Symbolic of remembrance and opening within.
My heart cries out to be more fully yours.
That all your beautiful qualities may be mine.

My Safe Haven

Past conversations, playing in my head,
Filled with negativity and anxiety
Are met with love and mercy.
God is everything and greater than my memories.
I will offer myself the same compassion
And encouragement that I give to others.
God is greater than my anxiety.
When I am afraid,
I will run with all of my heart
To the only one who can rescue and protect me
From my imaginings.
The lover of my soul is closer than my breath
And will never leave me without help.
God is greater than my fears.

When I am doubtful
Wandering through my life,
Feeling as though I have no course in mind:
As if there is no plan or relief,
I will fall into my heart to find the one,
Who knows what is best for me.
God is there,
Always as near to me as my heart itself.

The Lighthouse

The winding staircase inside of a lighthouse
Where each step is illuminated,
Leads toward the light which shines brightest.
This light can penetrate even the darkest night
It shines in the midst of a storm
To light the way to safety and peace.
It is the light by which I set my course.

The Dark Night of the Soul

I have heard that the "dark night of the soul"
Can descend like a curtain.
It is a time for your personal battle
Against doubts, fears, anger,
Or anything else that stands
Between you and the Lover of your soul.
It is the time to sort out the past
From the present,
A time to discern who you truly are.
Do not run in fear,
But treasure the time of discovery.
When the darkness is so deep
That you can scarce see your foot
Let alone, know where to put it,
Take heart.
Light returns, ever so gently at first.
As time progresses,
The light will ever increase,
Until you see that hope and love
Are what guide your path.
Mercy and compassion are ever your companions.
Such that when there is darkness
All around you, once again
The light from within will illuminate your path

The Light Within

When you look at me, you may see
An outer package which is unremarkable.
But deep within me, is
Something far greater than can be seen
With simple physical eyes.
Deep within, is a priceless jewel,
A light that the whole of the universe
Could not contain.
Within that light is endless love and mercy;
Endless compassion, forgiveness and grace.

You are my brother and sister.
We are progeny of the same parent.
The light that burns within me, is in you.
That great lover of our souls
Asks only that we return the love,
Not only to the source of all love,
But to the objects of that love.
Loving you is loving me is loving God within.
When all that is temporary disappears
That which is eternal will remain.
The source of all light and love:
The Creator is eternal.
We are one with the eternal ONE.

Draw Near

Draw near O Beloved.

                 Here am I my lover

Let me whisper words of love to you.

                 My heart receives you willingly.

Set aside all thoughts of other loves.

                 In you I delight.

Let our hearts beat as one.

                 Only you exist

You are mine and I am yours.

Nothing can stand between us.

                 I am totally surrendered to your love.

There is none whose love can match mine.

                 I knew not the meaning of love until I knew yours.

You will not be disappointed, O my dear one.

I Thirst

O my God, satisfy this thirst
Which only you can slake.
Grant me the peace
Which only you can supply.
Lift me up.
Let me drink deeply
Of your love, your mercy,
And your peace.

I am filled with your light
Which will never be extinguished,
Let me rest in the security of your protection.
It is your tender mercy that keeps me.
It is your love
That lifts me up.
I am drinking in your love.
Nothing else can quench my thirst.

Blessed Are They

It is easy to be kind to someone who loves you.
Be kind when someone is screaming at you.
Love the one who hates you.
A wounded animal bites.
Do not take it personally.
It is easy to give from your abundance.
Give then when you have little.
Generosity means something more then.
And what about giving to the person in need,
Who does not say thank you?
Are you giving for the "thanks"?
Or because it is the right thing to do?
How would you want to be treated?
Do not think too much of yourself.
You are no more or less than your neighbor.
Treat each person
As if God were wearing their skin
Regardless of how they behave.
Anyone can make war.
Be a peacemaker.
Hearts will open to you.

I am invited to swim in the ocean of God's love

When I Am Afraid

When I am afraid,
I believe I am alone in the world.
When I am afraid,
I feel helpless.
When fear overpowers me
I forget to think of anything
Except the fear that stands before me.
When I am afraid,
I don't see the angels watching over me.
When I am afraid,
I forget to call on
The One who can actually help me.
When I live in fear
I am conquered *in* my mind
And *by* my mind.
The illusion of separation from God,
Exists only within my thoughts.
God never left.
My fear created forgetfulness.
God is the Sustainer
The Ever-present Protector and Helper.

Seeing Beyond Illusion

As fog creeps up the hill
It disguises my view.
Though my vision may be obscured
Truth remains steadfast,
Even when not outwardly perceived.

The Generosity of God

Turn. O turn away from selfishness.

Understand with new eyes what your actions bring.

Extend a hand of mercy,

Even as mercy has been offered to you.

Be generous and non-judgmental.

God's generosity is unfathomable.

He gives without limits.

Judge not. But be generous to all.

Do not think for a moment that your riches

Can bring you happiness or peace of mind.

Peace comes from God.

All that you have is from the hand of God.

Embody the generosity of God.

Offer His love freely.

Give of your time and compassion.

His, is a good cause.

What is God's desire?

That you give of yourself with love and mercy.

That you surrender to God's compassionate heart.

That your heart and God's are as one.

"If you contribute to other people's happiness, you will find the true goal,
the true meaning of life."
His Holiness the XIVth Dalai Lama

Food for Thought

The flower bestows the sweetness of its life-giving nectar,
Offering the pleasant perfume of its wholesomeness.
Its fragrance invites all to drink deeply of its virtues.
Walk in God's garden and partake of the richness.

Thank You God

I had a difficult day at work today.
Thank you Lord.
You are the one I call upon for help.

I ate nutritious meals today.
Thank you God. You are the Provider.

I am learning to see your hand in everything.
Thank you God, You are the Awakener.

You show me the path to walk
Thank you God, You are the Light

When my path is uneven and
My course difficult, thank you God.
You are the Sustainer.

I arrived safely home.
In you, anywhere is home.
Thank you God.

"Verily, Allah (God) is the All-Provider." Qur'an 51:58

I Have Judged You

I have judged you,
Though not for any real offense.
I have judged you
Because you do not dress like me.
You do not look like me.
You are not the same gender or age as me.
Your skin does not look like mine.
You don't speak the same language
Nor do you pray the way I do.
When I look at you I am afraid.
I am told that people of your age are inconsiderate.
You don't understand the way things really are.
I am told that all people who speak your language;
Everyone who looks like you is violent.
I heard that everyone from your country
Is a drug dealer.
And I believed it,
Though not because of anything you have actually done.

I have judged you because you are not me.
I have treated you without respect.
I have harmed your spirit.
I have hindered your growth and I have kept you poor
And abused you.
I have justified my actions, because you are not me.
I have judged you, and yet it is me who should be judged.

Forgive me, please. I have offended you.
You are just like me.
You have a family and want to help them.
You need shelter from the storm
And food to fill your stomach.

Your clothes may be different
But they are merely coverings.
You require meaningful work
And you desire to be valued.
We may not always agree on everything,
But what family never has disagreements?
And you are my family member.
You and I are both human.
Therefore we are of one family.
Your God is one of love. Mine is too.
It is the same God. (There's only one.)

Please God, forgive me.
I have judged and acted without love.
Teach me to see myself in everyone.
Teach me to see *your face* in everyone.
Help me to offer love and mercy always,
So that I may not judge;
And that I may not *be* judged.

A Mirror Image

When I look in the mirror
Who is looking back at me?
Is it merely an image?
And who does God see
When He looks at me?
Does God see me in all my faults?
Or does He see all my potentials?
Perhaps God sees a finished being
And appreciates the process of being there.
When I look in the mirror
Can I be a little less critical of myself
And begin to see a finished work in progress?
Can I begin to see God in me,
And offer myself love accordingly?
What does God see when He looks at me?
God sees Himself.
The rest is illusion.

An End to Selfishness

I long to set aside the little ego.
My heart cries out
To see the end of pettiness,
To be one with the ONE.
Cover my eyes my beloved,
With your light.
Deafen my ears
To every voice but yours.
That seeing I might see
And hearing, I might truly hear.

Unless the Lord builds the house, its builders labor in vain.
The Bible, Psalm 127:1

Return to Me

Let down your veils my beloved
No more shall you hide yourself from me.
We shall stand together uncovered,
We who know each other
With the truth of our love.
I have known you before the invention of time.
You and I are as one my love.
Remember our union.

Return to me my beloved.
Understand your full potential.
Open to me, that we may once again
Be one in experience, knowledge and love.
The distance between us is illusion.
Veils without substance separate us.
Remember me. I have not changed.
You have forgotten the wonders of our love.

Let down your veils my beloved
And return to being as we once were.
Return to the state of knowing
When you and I heard each other's thoughts.
I hear you, but you have forgotten me.
You wonder through your life
In a state of loneliness and loss.
I am here my beloved.

Selah…Listen to my voice and remember.

I have never lost track of you
But you have forgotten our state of bliss.
You have forgotten our bond.

You have forgotten that
I have been the source of every good thing in your life.
Patiently, I await your amnesia to fall away.
Patiently, I call your name
With hope that your consciousness will return
To the reality of our unity.

Look within to find God's illumination

Moving Toward Life

Moving to rhythms of life
Senses are of limited value
Thoughtless in mind
Surrender
Deeper within
Into the stillness
Dying to deception
Opening to truth
Light and love without end
The Beloved with whom there are no barriers
Resting in the "Is"
One

From Deep Within

There is an artesian well of love
Which bubbles up from deep within
Unbidden, spontaneous.
It comes from the source of all love,
Nourishing the heart to bloom.

The path of love is not revealed
By merely reading any book.
Nor can a relationship be developed
By listening to sermons.
This certainty is not translated
Through ceremony or wand.

This path is recognized
With a spark of the knowledge of truth,
Smoldering until the spirit
Kindles the element of love and longing,
Creating a tempest which cannot be extinguished.

This life of passion
Cannot be transferred to another
By willing it to occur.
The thirsty individual seeking identity
Will fan the flames of eternity within
To discontinue time and space
Achieving transmutation of reality.

In The Mind of God

In the Mind of God, There Is Only Now.
Everything that has ever happened is occurring now.
Everything that will ever be
Is now.
All of my potential exists at this moment
Within the mind of God.
All of my accomplishments are present
Within the mind of God.
Everything that is, was, or ever will be
Exists here… now.
All that I possess is here… right now.
The essence of my being is… now.
God is all that ever was, is, or will be.
No other moment,
No other being has ever,
Nor will ever exist beyond now.
Time is deception.

Only God is.
In the breathless moment
God is.
In the silence between life and death,
God is.
In the place that has no manifestation
God is.
In the soundless, wordless thought
God is.
In the unity of all things,
GOD IS.

Looking Within

The flower bud opens, revealing its inner beauty.
Like the blossom, as we open our hearts
To the living God,
We begin to see the inner beauty;
The spark of God's light,
A core of God's mercy.
Compassion and love existing within.

How Time Flies

Where did it all go?
I thought I had so much more to spend.
I used it on those and that
Thinking there would always be more.
And now it is all gone.
And what have I left to show
For my wild outflows?
Would thriftiness have changed anything?
Time is a curious ingredient of life.
It is often treated as though
There is enough to waste.
And then one day we ask
Where have all the years gone?

If today, I sit all day in prayer or meditation,
Is that a better use than service to others?
And what if I devote my days to study?
Solving all of the mysteries of my world
Does not feed the poor.
Am I a spendthrift when
Observing the cares of others?
When am I wasting time?
And when am I investing it in the future?

And what is the future in which I must invest?
Do my actions today
Change the outcome of tomorrow?
Does investing time in compassion
Change the phases of the world?
There is only a limited amount
Of this precious resource
Available to every life form.
And yet, in truth… **Time is a delusion**.

May the Peace of God Be Within You

You say that you come in the name of God
To destroy the unbelieving, to demand
Obedience to the One.
God did not appoint you as avenger to His Honor.
You cry out, "God is Greatest".
As though to justify ungodly acts
Of violence and hatred.
And yet the chapters of the Holy Book
Begin with, "In the name of God
The most Gracious, the most Merciful.
God *is* greatest of everything
And everyone.
His name is one of peace.
He admonishes us to extend hands
As well as hearts with peace and compassion.

Some would compel others to be like themselves.
But God says that none
Should be compelled to convert.
All must be allowed
To worship God as a choice.
You are not appointed judge and jury to condemn.
But you are commanded to demonstrate mercy.
God seeks the love and devotion of His people,
Not ignorant and blind service.
God does not call His people to be warriors.
He has angels to carry out His will.

We are willing slaves
Surrendered to His overwhelming love.
God desires that we emulate His compassion,
Giving to the poor, the widowed, and orphaned.
God calls us to return to Him
The love which is freely offered.

It is in our surrender to His love
That we are invited back into the garden
Where we will live in the beauty
And the peace of His presence.
In Him is peace, mercy, love and compassion.

The Path

You ask me to follow you
To not stray away from the path
To listen attentively to your guidance
And then you disappear from view
You become silent
And the path is difficult to find
Because it has become overgrown
With obstacles.

And then you show up again,
Telling me that the path is illuminated.
That the light which shines from within
Will help me to see the obstacles
For what they actually are.
They are gifts
With wisdom and insight imbedded.

I ask you the questions ever on my mind.
"Where are we going?
How will I know when I arrive?"
You smile at me with such love,
It is as though you hold a secret
You are anxious to reveal
But the time is not ripe.
"You will know when you get there,"
You answer.

God is Love

Would the God who loves without measure
Provide salvation
To only a small portion of the world
And discard all the rest?
Does it not seem credible that in every language,
In every corner of the world, and in every time,
God would find a way to restore humanity
To the former relationship with the Divine
Which was enjoyed
In another state of being?

There is only one God.
That is indisputable.
And all people, and all life forms
Are God's creation.
Would God condemn to eternal punishment,
Good people who have never heard
Of Jesus, Moses, Mohammad (p.b.u.t)?
God has spoken to all peoples in many ways
To call them back to Himself.
He calls us all back to love.

God is love. It is written in the Holy Books.
God is love. It is written in our hearts.
We are all brothers and sisters… family.
We are instructed to do only two things:
Be love and demonstrate love.
Love God with all of our being and
Love our neighbor as ourselves.

How can I then, stubbornly dig in my heels,
Refusing to be moved while insisting
Everything must be done my way?
Shall I hold on to past offenses and wounds?
Would I not be merely rolling
In the muck and the mire?

Put away old wounds.
Discard hatred and resentments of the past.
Walk in the love which offers peace
And forgiveness for past offenses.
Ask not that others worship the same way as you,
But pray that they may love God
And serve the ONE who loves all.

God invites us into the garden, where we are re-united
Together in His love.

Walking Among Giants

I walk among the giants.
Trees so tall and closely united
Block the sun with only sparkles of light
Falling on the path below.
These behemoths yield only slightly
In a dance with the elements of wind and light.
Periodically, I see the sky above me
As I crane my neck, contorting my body
To see their tops
I understand how jealously
They seek illumination from above.
It drives them to grow ever upward
Until they reach heights
That none thought possible.
O to be a giant sequoia or redwood.
They have nothing else to do
But to drink in the light.
They do not stumble in the half lit world
Seeking out the path.

Stuff and Commentary

It is amazing how many friends show up
When they perceive you have something
Which they want. Greed speaks volumes.
Like praying to Santa Claus,
They say, "God give me…blah, blah, blah".
Other times of the year
You are simply blamed
For all the difficulties in life.

I don't know that I could be
So patient with humanity.
It seems that many don't think about you
Until they want something.
Perhaps, it is because you can see
How things turn out in the end,
From the very beginning,
That you withhold judgment.

What I want most of all from you
Every moment of every hour of every day,
You already offer me freely,
Without my needing to ask.
It is your abundant love,
Unconditional and boundless.
Nothing else really matters.
The rest is just stuff and commentary.

Can We Talk?

Let's be clear about one thing:
I am here because I love you.
You have proven yourself to me.
You and I have walked through difficult times
together.
And each time,
I found greater clarity
And a deeper love
Developing between us,
At least on my part.
I know that you always loved me.

But some people tell me
That I have this whole thing wrong
In regard to this thing we have going.
They tell me that I should fear you;
No, "serve you with fear and trembling".
Now while I yield to you a great deal
In giving me direction,
Ultimately, I thought I always had a choice.
And I always assumed
That you liked the fact that I chose
To let you run the show.
If I had thought for a moment
That you simply wanted a slave…
Well, I wonder if my love for you
Would have developed into what it has.

According to Your Will

Oh my God, I know that you hold all things.
Nothing happens, without your knowledge.
All around me, I see suffering and chaos.
Will you not put an end to these things?

And yet, somehow I can have peace
In the ocean of your love.
It is in my surrender that I hear
Your voice of mercy and compassion.

If it is your will, bring healing.
Healing, true healing comes with renunciation.
I anticipate the day when all people
Will eagerly surrender to love.

From A Mother's Heart

Oh my God
Please don't take my child's life!
I could not live without him.
He is everything to me
Please return him to his mother's loving arms
In perfect health.

    Oh my God
    Please don't take my child.
    You don't need him.
    He is so young.
    Take my life instead.
    If you spare him
    I will be your slave
    For the rest of my life.
        Oh God!
        How can you do this to my son?
        How can you do this to me?
        I have tried to serve you all my life
        And now you want to take my son's life?
        Oh God, I can't do anything to stop you.
        You are so much greater than me.
        You who made the heavens and the earth,
        Give me back my son!
            Oh my God,
            You who created all things
            Created my son.
            You see my tears and know my suffering.

You love me and pour out your compassion.
Your children are suffering all over this world.
And you are the only one
That can end our suffering.
Help me walk this road.
I cannot walk it alone.
I need your presence to comfort my heart.

Oh my beloved God
I am nothing without you.
I surrender this to you.
I surrender everything to you
Because of your great wisdom, mercy, and love.
I offer you my son. He is yours.
He always was.
I am yours completely.
I can do nothing but love you
And wait for your tender mercies
To comfort me in my time of sorrow.
You are the giver of all that is good.
I know that if you take his life now
He will be with you forever.
And I will love you still.

Oh my beloved God,
I am your loving servant.
I yield to
Your will.

Seasons of Loving

When the sun shines,
Prepare your field.
When rains fall,
Seeds will grow.
At the appointed time
Bring in the harvest.
When the snow falls
Make snow men
To help you clear a path.
When the heart fills with joy
Dance or sing from your heart.
Laugh when your heart overflows.
Cry when you feel alone.
You will never cry.
Love surrounds you in every season.

Too much sun
May bring forgetfulness.
Too much rain
Can lead to overwhelm.
Great abundance prolonged
Needs to be accompanied by gratefulness
Lest we forget.
In long periods of cold
Remember the heat of passion
And the giver of mercy.

When great joy abounds
Share it with all.
Times of sadness and loss
Are treasures also.
Dance as though
Your life depends on it.
Remembered love
Creates balance.

I Am a Child of God

I am a child of God.
God who is King of all kings,
Lord of lords.
And that makes me special.
Though perhaps I have no esteem among men
I am a child of God.
And so are you.

I am a child of God,
Creator of all that is,
Majestic and Bountiful
Who extends kindness and mercy to all humanity.
I am a child of God.
And so are you.

I am a child of God
The Unifier of all people
The Source of all light
Who brings forth the truth of great love for all.
I am a child of God.
And so are you.

I am a child of God,
The Source of love,
Eternal and compassionate,
Offering limitless love to all of God's creations.
I am a child of God.
And so are you.

I am a child of God,
Who exists forever
At the core of my being.
We are all exceptional in God's sight.
I am a child of God.
And so are you.

I am a child of God
The Giver of Peace
Which rules my life.
God's is the peace beyond understanding.
I am a child of God.
And so are you.

You are a child of God,
The author of forgiveness,
Pardoning our thoughtlessness
God asks us to forgive one another also.
You are a child of God
And so am I.

Good-Bye

Good-bye my friend.
May you reach your destination
With ease of passage.
Fare well, my companion.
Go with God in peace.
Though you are out of my sight
You are ever in my heart.
May the distance between us
Be as nothing
Until that great day when we are reunited.
You will be missed my friend.
Gone but not forgotten.
We will see each other again some day
And the joy of our reunion will be great.
But until that day, good-bye.

There was a time, when traveling across continents meant that you would never see your loved one again. It was as though that one had died, though that was not necessarily true. That person could not be reached. The voice was no longer within hearing distance. The body was gone. Though the person continued, the loved one had ceased to exist in every-day life for those left behind. Is it any different in death? Though the voice cannot be heard and the body has ceased to be present, yet the loved one continues. The soul lives. Gone or simply gone from sight?

Lavender

Have you seen pictures of the fragrant flower, lavender?
When looking at a photo of the flower,
One might think that surely
If the blossom were ever encountered
You would be able to recognize it.
Have you ever smelled lavender?
There are many types of lavender.
Do they all smell the same?
Are they all still lavender?
Hold a blossom in your hand.
Squeeze it between your fingers.
Now you really know what lavender is all about.
The oil permeates your skin.
Walk through a field of lavender
Where the smell wafts into your nostrils.
All that you see around you is lavender
Each time you brush against a branch.
You can feel the essence of lavender
When you are surrounded by its perfume
You are experiencing lavender in a new way.

The Treasure Hunt

As a child,
I always loved treasure hunts.
I was given a list of articles
Which I was expected to find.
I think that I am on a treasure hunt now
To discover the qualities
Inherent in love.
My Beloved has given me a list.
Everything has been carefully written down
So that I might not forget even one element.
And now I am on a quest of discovery.
I will bring my treasures back to my Love,
Not carried in a bag to empty on the floor
As proof of my adventure.
They must instead, be returned to my Love
By opening my heart,
Revealing the jewels
Carefully nurtured within my soul.

Butterfly Wings

Lost in the ecstasy of your name
I explore the boundlessness of your love.
The world, even the universe disappears.
I am blanketed by you, cossetted.
I could stay forever in this state of bliss.
But I am bidden back to the flatness of the earth.

If the mere beating of a butterfly's wings
Could alter the course of the future
Or cause the wind to blow around the world,
What would happen if we all danced together in ecstasy?
How would the world be different
If we all joyously chanted your names in unison?
Perhaps if we would all laugh together
We could put an end to wars.

My Name is Joy

My mother named me Joy.
For years, I had no idea what that meant.
But now…
I AM JOY!!!
Joy is not only my middle name
It is the place I live.
Joy is a child I've chosen to adopt.
Joy comes from my heart.
It is a state of being
Which grows from knowing that
I AM LOVED!!!
This knowledge makes me smile.
Love gives me joy.

What is Joy?
A simple emotion?
Is it ecstasy?
Or is it a deep peace that keeps my soul safe,
Preventing it from being tossed by the storms?
I have been in the midst of storms.
I am still alive.
And God's love is still my refuge,
My shelter in the storm.
God is where I run for my life.
There is nothing else but God,
My source of joy.

God is love. I can't say it too much. The knowledge of God's love gives me such joy. Past suffering has been transformed by love. I will joyfully yield to the lover of my soul. Where love and trust abide, joy and peace are abundant.

Ms. Pennington graduated from Marylhurst University with a bachelor of arts degree in interdisciplinary studies. She then earned a master of divinity from the University of Metaphysical Sciences.

Ms. Pennington is married to her soul mate, Todd. She has grown children and several grandchildren.

Ms. Pennington and her husband enjoy exploring the Northwest and taking photos of the abundant beauty.

Printed in the United States
By Bookmasters